Also by Spencer Reece

THE CLERK'S TALE

THE ROAD TO EMMAUS

Spencer Reece

THE ROAD TO EMMAUS

Farrar Straus Giroux

New York

FARRAR, STRAUS AND GIROUX

18 West 18th Street, New York 10011

Printed in the United States of America

First edition, 2014

Grateful acknowledgment is made to the Estate of
Roberto Sosa for permission to translate "Los Pobres."

Library of Congress Cataloging-in-Publication Data

Reece, Spencer.

[Poems. Selections]

The Road to Emmaus / Spencer Reece. — First edition.

pages cm

ISBN 978-0-374-28085-7 (hardcover)

I. Title.

PS3618.E4354 A6 2014

811'.6—dc23

2013032997

Designed by Quemadura

Farrar, Straus and Giroux books may be purchased for
educational, business, or promotional use. For information
on bulk purchases, please contact the Macmillan Corporate
and Premium Sales Department at 1-800-221-7945,
extension 5442, or write to specialmarkets@macmillan.com.

www.fsgbooks.com
www.twitter.com/fsgbooks
www.facebook.com/fsgbooks

1 3 5 7 9 10 8 6 4 2

I dedicate this book to:

my father, Dr. Richard Lee Reece
my mother, Loretta Witkins Reece
my brother, Carter Straight Reece

&

Bishop Leo Frade & Dr. Diana Frade

—all my love,
all my gratitude to two families
who believed in me

The real difference between God and human beings, he thought, was that God cannot stand continuance. No sooner has he created a season of a year, or a time of the day, than he wishes for something quite different, and sweeps it all away. No sooner was one a young man, and happy at that, than the nature of things would rush one into marriage, martyrdom or old age. And human beings cleave to the existing state of things. All their lives they are striving to hold the moment fast, and are up against a force majeure. Their art itself is nothing but the attempt to catch by all means the one particular moment, one mood, one light, the momentary beauty of one woman or one flower, and make it everlasting. It is all wrong, he thought, to imagine paradise as a never-changing state of bliss. It will probably, on the contrary, turn out to be, in the true spirit of God, an incessant up and down, a whirlpool of change.

—ISAK DINESEN, ''THE MONKEY''

Contents

THE ROAD TO EMMAUS

ICU

Those mornings I traveled north on I-91,
passing below the basalt cliff of East Rock
where elms discussed their genealogies.
I was a chaplain at Hartford Hospital,
took the Myers-Briggs with Sister Margaret,
learned I was an *I* drawn to *E*s.
In small group I said, "I do not like it,
the way young black men die in the ER,
shot, unrecognized, their gurneys stripped,
their belongings catalogued and unclaimed."
In the neonatal ICU, newborns breathed,
blue, spider-delicate in nests of tubes.
A Sunday of themselves, their tissue purpled,
their eyelids the film on old water in a well,
their faces resigned in plastic attics,
their skin mottled mildewed wallpaper.
It is correct to love even at the wrong time.
On rounds, the newborns eyed me, each one
like Orpheus in his dark hallway, saying:
I knew I would find you, I knew I would lose you.

THE MANHATTAN PROJECT

First, J. Robert Oppenheimer wrote his paper on dwarf stars—"What happens to a massive star that burns out?" he asked. His calculations suggested that instead of collapsing it would contract indefinitely, under the force of its own gravity. The bright star would disappear but it would still be there; where there had been brilliance there would be a blank. Soon after, workers built Oak Ridge, the accumulation of Cemesto hutments not placed on any map. They built a church, a school, a bowling alley. From all over, families drove through the muddy ruts. The ground swelled about the ruts like flesh stitched by sutures. My father, a child, watched the loads on the tops of their cars tip. Gates let everyone in and out with a pass. Forbidden to tell anyone they were there, my father's family moved in, quietly, behind the chain-link fence. Niels Bohr said: "This bomb might be our great hope." My father watched his parents eat breakfast: his father opened his newspaper across the plate of bacon and eggs, his mother smoked Camel Straights, the ash from her cigarette cometing across the back of the obituaries. They spoke little. Increasingly the mother drank Wild Turkey with her women friends from the bowling league. Generators from the Y-12 plant droned their ambition. There were no birds. General Leslie Groves marched the boardwalks, yelled, his boots pressed the slates and the mud bubbled up like viscera. My father watched his father enter the plant. My shy father went to the library, which was a trailer with a circus tent painted on the side. There he read the definition of "uranium," which was worn to a blur. My father read one Hardy Boys mystery after another. It was August 1945. The librarian smiled sympathetically at the twelve-year-old boy. "Time to go home," the librarian said. They named the bomb Little Boy. It weighed 9,700 pounds. It was the size of a go-kart. On the battle cruiser *Augusta*, President Truman said, "This is the greatest thing in history." That evening, my father's parents mentioned Japanese cities. Everyone was quiet. It was the quiet of the exhausted and the innocent. The quietness inside my father was building and would come to define him. I was wrong to judge it. Speak, Father, and I will listen. And if you do not wish to speak, then I will listen to that.

MONACO

Monaco was clean, with small clean streets.
There was not much in the way of a shore.
There was hardly any place to go.
How feminine the tiny cityscape was—
all whimsical curves and dark, rich cul-de-sacs.
So unlike Corsica, its coarse cousin nearby—
an island of Mafia, sharp rocks,
and hairy wild boars that twitched like genitals.

Delicate Monaco,
how on earth did you protect yourself?
Before the Ansbacher bank office,
one clipped, well-behaved London plane tree,
not welcoming like ordinary trees,
was kept apart by a white spear-tipped fence,
and had a somewhat diffident sense of noblesse oblige.
Through the cream silk brocade window treatments,
you could see it: it did not contain birds,
repelled the idea of nests, its roots
trained and snipped. At night, it was lit.
Winds shook the leaves like a showgirl's tassels.
In the palace hung a portrait of Princess Grace's family,

an extravaganza of pastel sfumato by R. W. Cowan,
blurring every frail, authentic thing.
Surrounded by high cliffs,
the air in the principality backed up like in a closet.
Lovers smooched on the embankment.
The night cross-dressed into dawn.

When the man and woman arrived at the Hôtel de Paris,
the staff assumed they were married.
The German Jet Ski instructor was unsure
and asked: "Are you brother and sister?"
They paused, demurely, and smiled.
The mystery of their bond intensified it.
The man and woman were in their late thirties
or early forties; they were not young nor were they old.

The woman was French and wore a white linen shirt,
starched and pressed. She made her money in the drug trade
(laundering money from the sale of cocaine or heroin
until the money became unrecognizably clean),
but all the man knew was that she sold works of art:
a Matisse here, a Picasso there—
her transactions often involving a visit to the Bahamas.
She was what she said she was.
But we are rarely what we say we are.

They met at a sales counter in Palm Beach

where the man was ringing up items at 75 percent off each.

She invited him on a trip,

after she gave him a sizeable tip.

The man, a poor American,

meant to say no, but agreed instead.

Tall, athletic, effeminate, with a mincing gait,

he looked as if he were being chased

by something no one could see.

He wore needle-pointed shoes by Stubbs & Wootton

and dressed in cashmere and shantung.

The broad-shouldered Frenchwoman grimaced,

was referred to as "handsome."

Ample her gestures, ample her need to please;

if her tone was not sexual, it came close.

The couple exhibited variations

the world never embraced, but presented as a couple

the world embraced promptly,

for the world trusted what was coupled.

Both controlled their wonder.

Whatever their motives,

the naïveté they displayed hid their intentions.

Skirting promises at a café, she asked:

"What shall we name our children, *mon petit cheri*?"

They made a myth for everyone to see.

One day, similar to all their days,

the couple went to the Casino in Monte Carlo.

There they met the androgynous Baroness von Lindenhoffer.

Many proposed the baroness was lesbian,

but of this she never spoke.

Some believed her to be a conundrum—

her muteness alluding perhaps to a hidden passion

or a complicated reaction to herself

for reasons long forgotten or buried.

This might have been true, but just as probable,

some thought her shy,

an unsuccessful heterosexual who was deeply mannish.

Moving about imperiously in black patent leather high-heeled
   shoes

custom-made for her large feet,

she exuded isolation as if it were a scent.

Something inside her had ceased.

Even if all sexualities fail,

the baroness, in this regard, was magnificent.

The Frenchwoman sold the baroness a Toulouse-Lautrec.

Receiving the couple for cakes and tea,

the baroness wrote out her check

and began a conversation about her brief marriage

to a hairy Russian acrobat. Her makeup was heavy

as a clown's, and a red polka-dotted muumuu

sheeted her large, ill-defined parts.

Beneath her muumuu her many crevices were compacted with
talc.

Yet despite efforts to look and smell womanly,

people mistook her for a man.

When she answered the phone in her plummy alto,

her posh English accent was influenced by German,

so words would be disguised by *v*s and *z*s.

To the caller, she said: "No, I am a *v*oman."

On a chintz love seat, each hip bookended by a pug,

she sat and said: "You *z*eem a lovely couple!"

She meant what she said

but she did not say what she meant.

Then there was talk of places they had traveled

and feelings of superiority

at having seen what others had not:

"Oh, you haven't been there?" and "Oh, you must go!"

Through the large picture window,

beyond the baroness's head,

piled high with hair dyed red,

gargantuan cruise ships were set on the Monegasque sea

like wedding cakes with glittering tiers of candles.

From the baroness's earlobes, hanging low,

her Verdura eardrops made of peridot,

so that when she laughed her deep upper-class laugh—
Hardee-har-har! and *Tee-hee-hee!*—
her head tinkled like a chandelier in an earthquake.
She had the cultivated dignity of those
who withhold their lives.
Inserting another biscotto behind her lips
which were puffed up and shaped not unlike luggage handles,
she winked like someone on the make
(but on the make for what?),
and said, sotto voce: "Here in Monaco our favorite *v*ord is
   'more'!"

The couple scanned the shore's shuttered clutter—
the sea published its gossip,
flashed its gilded mirrors.
The sun accelerated beauty and its loss.
No children for miles and beyond, down the Côte d'Azur,
Brigitte Bardot, in St.-Tropez, locked her house,
cats licking her purple-veined ankles.

Behind her coffee table
upon which bonbons were displayed,
the baroness finished the story of her life as a wife.
She expanded her chest like a concertina,
memory enlivening her,

her eyes fixed in surprise with Botox.
In a look from history's unwritten side,
she attempted to be sentimental and failed.
She paused like an old steamer.
Spangled and remote, her mascara-clotted eyelids closed.
Should she warn the couple?
Although questionably feminine, she was maternal.
Then that thought, or half-thought, passed.

The baroness shrugged
with the weight of candy and age.
She had become what she had become.
She thanked the couple, admired her new purchase.
Already she felt the hint of boredom with them
and began to anticipate their imminent expulsion.
Straightening her body's luggage,
a final time she assessed the couple of ambitious compromises,
aware that nothing stains the heart like a *mariage blanc*,
and stamped them—*Mwah! Mwah!*—
with the imprimatur of two kisses each.

The couple stood like marionettes,
left after a promise to rendezvous—
the absence of conviction was not missed by the three.
Under a royal-blue awning,

behind a marble balustrade,

past croquet wickets and phallic topiary,

beyond red berries cracked with sugar,

the baroness diminished in the couple's vision.

They could just make out her muffled laughter

as she chatted to a maître d'

about the men she wished to date.

And when at last the baroness was alone,

melancholy molded her the way night molds Paris:

she retreated into her cold hole,

dropped her pretenses,

once more accepted her solitary role,

and removed her girdle, bra, and panties.

The elastics, straps, and clasps

had left imprinted welts on her skin

that looked like a series of scars and stitches.

Her flesh was released. She sighed.

She farted.

And there she stood, sagging like an old cathedral.

The couple did not last.

Having chosen wrongly, plausibly, they fell apart,

like the couple in Godard's *Le Mépris*.

Their time ended

after a spat at the Hôtel du Cap.

Or was it a kiss in the Boboli Gardens?

Had she wanted more than a cover?

Had he covered more than he'd wanted?

How faceted, coveted, and intricate, the heart!

Behind its casements,

fixed in its singular setting, who owns it?

He could not be kept.

She withdrew her money.

On their last night in Monaco, she turned to him

and wondered if her life had meant anything.

He did not answer.

He had offered himself to someone who found truth difficult,

which required one to abide and be circumspect,

for is not the truth ugly, more often than not?

(The truth, what is the truth?)

When they left the restaurant, she paid

using a heavy black American Express card.

Each took a doggy bag and smelled of cooked meat.

This alignment of opposite sexes

had provided solace, and for a time,

each had assumed a place, discerned a way to live.

They lived on,

both aware the one had altered the other:

whether intended or not,

the act could not be undone.

What they recalled, when they recalled it,

was often wrong, or was it that so much went wrong

and that was why they kept recalling?

At the mention of Monaco, they recounted adornment—

the agapanthus bursting in fists of amethyst, old men playing
   boules,

and blue yachts tilting on a malachite sea,

or were they malachite yachts tilting on a blue sea?

Wherever they went afterwards,

their minds would sometimes fall on Monaco

and their encounter with the androgynous baroness.

Monaco, Monaco—

frivolous, ridiculous, minuscule.

Was it there they came to know danger,

how one could disappear into a beautiful lie?

There were lies in their truth

and truth in their lies—

sometimes to love is to lie and to lie

is to love. Each, in their separate lives,

mentioned Monaco with deference, out of shyness,

yes, but also shame, and that need

to abridge the past. Do you recognize them?

They were not a couple, but they were a pair.

Tonight,

the sea pushes against Monaco.

Jewelry-store owners lock their doors,

don white gloves

to lay the polished gems down in long green felt trays,

sheeting them with a placating, measured hush—

the way one lays orphans down to sleep in an orphanage.

In a grand, drafty hallway,

the baroness has had her portrait painted and affixed to a wall.

The paint has halted her age, softened her sex.

On her balcony,

she can see the narrow, dead-end streets

embed themselves like bobby pins

holding the escarpments and shrubbery in place

like wigs. She has forgotten the couple.

In the dark,

hotels, banks, and the Casino shrink.

Transient, glamorous,

the moon spreads her cape of baubles across the sea,

leaning over the dollhouses that make up Monaco,

lighting up each rich subject,

feeling into the rooms,

fingering the miniatures.

THE FIFTH COMMANDMENT

Waiting with an unfinished, finished look
behind honeysuckles that crown Old Saybrook,
she is reading Vita Sackville-West,
he has food on his moth-eaten sweater vest.
Here's the Oriental rug, still steeped in piss
from their bulldog who barked like an activist.
She seems happy, reigning with creams you FedExed,
rubbing his scalp, patched with scabby flecks
(as his squamous-cell carcinomas sprout,
the local dermatologist cuts them out
or frosts the growths with liquid nitrogen).
Tonight they talk of their last vegetable garden,
count out their pills in chipped cereal bowls
(you know the ones), check their sugar levels,
bicker over books misplaced, tchotchkes
lost, their tongues like well-used church keys.
Brother, last night half the garden nearly froze.
The dash between their dates is nearly closed.

GILGAMESH

Fragments

I

We lived on a lake with Muscovy ducks.
Weekly, they reproduced whole neighborhoods.
I saw them thrust with the thrust of youth.
Interior decorators flush with furniture plans,
arranging and rearranging,
collecting their fragments,
as if constantly preparing to marry.

Their flamboyant army flocked their barracks
with the panache of Frank Gehry.
Yes, they were certain about their truth.

Jerking the lake's surface with their agendas,
sometimes the ducks fought.
Smooth and polite above the waist,
beneath the lake,
their lower extremities displayed private panic

and that fear we recognized
of being caught.

But all is to be dared, because . . .

II

    Fragments, clay cylinders, tablets, parchment—
to write Genesis, they say, the writers
searched their neighborhood,
found all kinds of things, including
the epic about Gilgamesh, much of it damaged,
regarding the man who saw into the deep.

    Somehow, the part
about Gilgamesh and Enkidu
in love
got lost.

III

Once, two men,
Joseph and Spencer,
met at the gay community center,
called Compass, in Lake Worth,
which sponsored the Coming Out Group,
with Forest, their skilled leader.
In the group they used first names
like when you are part of a family.

Transsexuals met before.
Joseph was fifty, Spencer thirty-nine—
somewhat late to begin a life together
for the first time.

The New York Times has begun announcing
the unions of men.

Now they knew
it was possible to repeat
without being beaten or imprisoned:
"Joseph O'Shaughnessy and Spencer Reece were joined . . ."

Five years they had,
meeting on their celery-green love seat.
Not forever.
But something.

Something still.

IV

There were lulls.

We played Scrabble:
I arranged the tiles and you kept score.
Sometimes we rolled the dice and read the *I Ching*.
We went about our days unseen
and we loved that.
I placed too many books against the walls:
Capote, *Madame Bovary*, a biography of Anne Boleyn,
and Ross MacDonald mysteries,
some I'd read twice, some twice and slow.

Looking at the books, I thought:
Literature, like religion,
often needs death to grow.

You complained:
"Where will guests put their suitcases?"

We squabbled about money.
Often, you stretched out
on the double bed, your skin no longer young,
pebbled, freckled,
known by me.

V

The city was jammed under Joseph's nails
from construction work,
calloused hands that knew bar joists.
His was an Irish body,
inherited from parents whose bodies were punished
by the tin-colored rains around Croagh Patrick—
no food and poverty, a relative said:
"County Mayo is pretty all right, but you can't eat scenery."
Joseph was a tough guy from Brighton,
a tough neighborhood.

Beyond him, manatees,
scared by propellers,
huddled in the power plant's warm waters.
Palm fronds shook as wildly as pornography.

In the news,
a chimpanzee had ripped off a woman's face,
pulled her face and hands
off like tender petals.

VI

Forest provided them with fragments
to teach them how to live.
One text began: "God,
help me let go of my fears
and shame around my sexuality."

On the edges of our dreams was the sea;
there the moon walked,
her soft footsteps falling all over her neighborhood.

The juice of us dripped
on our hands and feet like candle wax.

The moon said:
"All your life you have waited for this,
this is what you wanted."

VII

Our dog, a Lab mix named Butch,
chewed a bone at your bare feet.
Butch moved like a shadow
on the sea's floor. Big and black,
he came to us abused—
who willingly destroys
and why does destruction last?

The drugged chimpanzee
had slept in the same bed as the neighbor.

We fed Butch a daily Xanax tablet
before he pulled us
on his manic journeys that had no end.

VIII

When we visited your aunt Annie
in the Needham nursing home outside Boston,
her walker dominated the room
like an empty kennel.
She did not know who I was;
each visit she gave me a different name.

African nurses from Nigeria
chitchatted about celebrities,
moving in their blueberry gowns and tangerine plastic clogs—
exotic fish, schooling in America.

When your mother died,
your father, who worked in the shipyards,
sent a letter
and a photograph of the four children to Killeen,
asking Aunt Annie to come.

"Please come, Annie, please come . . ."

As she strove across the sea,
she watched the Connemara ponies disappear,
then Knock, Letterfrac, Roundstone,
and Cashel Bay blurred, blurred,
blurred until they were nothing but green.
Ireland, that nation of neighborhoods, receded.
She left for good and raised you
and your three sisters:
Joan, Ann, and Maureen.

But all is to be dared because . . .

In Boston,
she went about her days unseen.
On her day off, she lit four candles,
one for each child,
at the Shrine of St. Anthony on Arch Street.
She adored you.
She never married.

When we visited,
she kept saying in her lilting Irish accent,
more song than talk:

"Joseph, Joseph, I have to get the cows across the stream."

IX

On Pelican Lake in Juno Beach,
caregivers and patients from the Alzheimer's Support Group
commenced their semi-detached dates,
eating potato chips off paper plates,
feeding their broken bits to the ducks.
Such was our neighborhood.

Eyes vacantly connected
where born-agains with failed marriages sent pamphlets
to Jews so they could be saved by Christ:
to conquer and subdue seemed to be Florida's forte.

The two men napped.
The ducks strutted,
preened their greasy black-green plumes,
shook their mashed red-crayon pates.
Developers demanding more room, the ducks were sated,
companioned, unbundling their poop.

I read Benjamin Britten's biography:
what motivated him to compose "Abraham and Isaac"
was neither the Bible nor World War II,
but rather his love of young boys: having power
over them was a lifelong passion
tolerated by Peter Pears, his companion.
Once finished, I placed the book against the wall.
A chorus of the dead began to surround us.
How to distinguish between life and art?

In the hospital, the reports said,
a veil was placed over the head
of the woman without a face,
as Zeus had done to Hera before their marriage vow.
Nurses feathered the woman with gauze,
dabbing her wounds with ointment.

X

That last time we visited Aunt Annie
we'd begun to have trouble,
your silence rendering you
a kind of stranger,
your Christ-kiss issuing no more,
and the gradual withdrawal of your touch
had begun to remove the clock's face and hands.

A retired couple volunteered,
instructing residents in the tango:
the lady had stained white tights,
the man a tambourine. The tango emoted
from the boom box as the residents gathered
in a crescent moon of wheelchairs
to make a kind of neighborhood.

Out the sealed windows,
Boston remained muzzled.
Dorchester and Brighton a series of cages.

Aunt Annie talked about her cows, the stream.
We stood behind her like groomsmen.

XI

In Juno Beach, in a drawer,
I found the calling cards you'd collected—
Tatoobody and Surferboy—
escorts, like racehorses one might bet on.

You love me. You love me not.
You love me. You love me not.

In the secret Gospel of Mark,
a man called the beloved disciple
flees the scene of a one-night stand with Christ,
smelling of the Zeus-juice of love,
and wanders the streets of his neighborhood.

When they bound the Bible,
this got lost.

XII

". . . no, I do not desire him,"
Joseph said to the therapist. Always honest,
your Boston accent hammered the syllables,
lathed the ends of words, so desire became "desi-*uh*"
(a neighbor thought I lived with a gangster).

"I want a younger man,
between the ages of twenty and twenty-five."

"What happens when he turns twenty-six?"

"I'll find a new one."

Like a mystery novel reaching its tight conclusion,
Joseph wanted predictable suspense.

Outside the office, the day blued.
I could hear our book of changes closing.

Our therapist proposed
an open marriage:
we could ape a romance instead of have one.

"I can't . . . No, no . . . I can't . . ."

The therapist looked noncommittal,
like a neighbor one doesn't know well.

Perhaps losing his mother so young,
I suggested to Forest, the Coming Out Group leader,
had made Joseph determined never to get too close.
That is why he needed a love in captivity.
I had begun to guess at things.

But all is to be dared because . . .

You were what you had always been,
only more so,
Irish and unavailable, darling.

Darling . . .

XIII

As I began to pack up my books,
you adored me still and I loved you still.
Strange.

The horizon handsawed through the house.
I could not sleep or read. The ducks quack-quacked,
copulating into oblivion as if sex were religion.
When I could not reach what I loved,
the world was rent. I waited until 6 AM.
Then I rang my parents, they
whose marriage I had judged harshly,
and they said:

"*Come home . . . Come home . . .*"

"I do not understand poetry,"
Joseph often said. "What's the point?"
(This charmed me, as if poetry,
like religion, is a mystery.)

The day I left, and the day after . . .

I rented a little room in our neighborhood.
Joseph wanted to see me still, but I could not.

"Why can't we be friends?"

I began to write this poem,
employing his real name. I suppose,
as a way of talking to him.
A poem, I thought, is not a fiction.

"You can't use his real name,"
a member from the Coming Out Group said.
"It's cruel. He's not out. He's not dead."

Where does biography end?

Where does poetry start?

How to construct the architecture of the heart?

"Kindness, kindness matters," my mother said.

XIV

Some things cannot be contained in a zoo.

I kept my name; I changed yours.

I began to dwell once more in uncertainty.

Joy would return, I knew, but when?
A friend had a stillborn child,
and her marriage ended.
She did not name the infant.
We had coffee at the Greek restaurant in our neighborhood.
She talked of going back to teach at Dreyfoos,
the arts high school, and one student, in particular,
a gay boy with acne who dreamt of a way out,
Juilliard.

Florida luxuriated out the window:
the firebush, the cornflower-blue plumbago,
the Mexican petunia.

Enkidu died.

The woman without a face
had a tracheotomy.
She spoke to the reporters
through a spokesperson and said:

"A little while and you will see me."

Seagulls diminished,
gray specks, gray motes.
The therapist in Fort Lauderdale
made no more appointments for the two men.

Migrant day laborers out in Pahokee and Canal Point
on Lake Okeechobee gleaned
and went about their days unseen.
The orange groves' fragile hemispheres
wobbled on their stems. Sugarcane fields burned.
Electrical poles gleamed.
Buck hoists and bucket trucks
broke through the possum's sedge.
The Coming Out Group took on new members.
Tadpoles expressed their sexualities,
opening their crotches like Bibles.
The Everglades sighed.
Extinction was in the air.

But all is to be dared because . . .

Mr. Reece sold his library, his piano.
He boarded a train and for a time
he returned to the edge of his parents' neighborhood.
Limitations present their possibilities.

The Guggenheim Bilbao
designed by Frank Gehry shines by the water
like a duck collecting fragments.
Early on, Gehry's wife made him change his last name,
which had been Goldberg.
There are many reasons we change the truth—
art, love, fear, hate, shame—
and the more love there is
the more they seem the same.

XVI

Aunt Annie lost her index finger
in Coventry,
during the Blitz.

Repeatedly
she rubbed the stump.

XVII

Perhaps Joseph walks now
there, with his young men, St. Augustine grass
under their feet, meaty with desire.
Undetected, perhaps they speak
of dissatisfactions, of politics.

Gilgamesh, his wedding off,
searched and searched
beneath the waters for what would not die.

The Atlantic—
narrowing to a flushed, sanguine strip,
fishing boats alone in the dark—
murmuring,
hooking,
perhaps young men love you,
plead with you:

"Stay . . . Stay . . ."

Perhaps the young
lay themselves down
as Isaac did for Abraham.
I-95 and A1A pulsing like blood
down the spits of Palm Beach County,
perhaps your face tightens tenderly
in response to what they say,
what you see.

AT THOMAS MERTON'S GRAVE

We can never be with loss too long.
Behind the warped door that sticks,
the wood thrush calls to the monks,
pausing atop the stone crucifix,
singing: "I am marvelous alone!"
Thrash, thrash goes the hayfield:
rows of marrow and bone undone.
The horizon's flashing fastens tight,
sealing the blue hills with vermilion.
Moss dyes a squirrel's skull green.
The cemetery expands its borders—
little milky crosses grow like teeth.
How kind time is, altering space
so nothing stays wrong: and light,
more new light, always arrives.

MARGARET

I remember she rented a room on the second floor from Jenny
Holtzerman, an Austrian widow. The two women lived on Gi-
rard Avenue South, in Kenwood, an elegant neighborhood of
Minneapolis. Any promise of husbands had disappeared long
ago. From the kitchen I often remember the jelly smell of a
Linzer torte. I was in high school and often eavesdropped.
Once, quietly, she said to my mother, "I never knew the love
of a man." She spoke English with an Eastern European heav-
iness, the vowels thick as dumplings, weighed down by history,
or was it disappointment? She had mentioned having a hus-
band, but during the war they were separated in the chaos of
Budapest, and later she lost track of him. Once she showed
me her room: the walls were bare with cracks. Her daybed was
narrow, barely slept in. Her room resembled hundreds of
scant little rooms around the world, the way it accepted blue
and purple-violet detail—on her bureau, no family photo-
graphs, instead playbills autographed by cast members, a
calendar tattered, crossed, marked, no jewelry, some coins.
Her window sashes warped, her wires shorted, and the paint
around her doorframe kept chipping off—"like in *The Cherry
Orchard*," she said, "by Chekhov." She told a joke in Hungar-
ian to Hannah Tamasek, and even *I*, not knowing a word,

laughed. When she said the word "America," she did so with a tone one associates with sacred things. She bowed gently in a manner distinctly Viennese and spoke on occasion of the Austro-Hungarian Empire. She loved the Guthrie Theater, where curtains rose on miniature worlds, preferring memorized dialogue and costumes to something truer. Five feet tall in orthopedic shoes, she limped. Time has a way of rearranging things and I could have most details wrong now, but there was this: during the war, she met a man, to whom she gave money, she did not know the man well, but had trusted him to smuggle her father across the border, the man pocketed the money, bought chocolates for his mistress from Belgium, and placed Margaret's father on a train to Auschwitz. So it makes sense to me now that simple decisions baffled Margaret. It makes sense to me now that when news reached us of Primo Levi's suicide, Margaret did not blink. It makes sense to me now that when Dr. Sikorski spoke of fighting in the Warsaw sewers, Margaret said: "I do not believe in God." Those who saw what they saw grow fewer. Margaret has been dead a long time now. But perhaps you will understand why I chose her, why I smudged the slow waltz of her smile, adding a few strokes, here and here. As you leave Margaret behind and turn the page, listen as the page falls back and your hand gently buries her. This is what the past sounds like.

1 CORINTHIANS 13

How long do we wait for love?
Long ago, we rowed on a pond.
Our oars left the moon broken—
our gestures ruining the surface.
Our parents wanted us to marry.
Beyond the roses where we lay,
men who loved men grew wounds.
When do we start to forget our age?
Your husband and I look the same.
All day, your mother confuses us
as her dementia grows stronger.
Your boys yell: *Red Rover!*
We whisper your sister's name
like librarians; at last on the list,
her heart clapping in her rib cage,
having stopped now six times,
the pumps opened by balloons,
we await her new heart cut
out from the chest of a stranger.
Your old house settles in its bones,
pleased by how we are arranged.

Our shadow grows like an obituary.
One of us says: "It is getting so dark."
Your children end their game.
Trees stiffen into scrapbooks.
The sky's shelves fill with stars.

THE ROAD TO EMMAUS

For Nathan Gebert

I

The chair from Goodwill smelled of mildew.
I sat with Sister Ann, a Franciscan,
in her small office, at the Cenacle Retreat House,
right on South Dixie Highway in Lantana, Florida,
and began my story—
it was an interview, much of life is an interview.
She said I did not need to pay her, but donations,
yes, donations were appreciated:
they could be left anonymously in a plain white envelope
that she could take back to the cloister.
She was dressed in a turtleneck and a denim jumper.
She could have been mistaken in a grocery store for an aging
    housewife.
My meetings with her went on a few years.

I had come to speak about Durell.
I did not know how to end my sentences about Durell.
He had taught me . . . what? To live? Not to wince in the mirror?

What? There were so many ways to end my sentence.

He was an unlikely candidate for so many things.

Outside, it was always some subtle variation of summer.

I paused, then spoke urgently, not wanting to forget some fact,

but much I knew I would forget, or remember in a way my own,

which would not exactly be correct, no, not exactly.

Durell was dead, I said, and I needed to make sense of things.

Sister Ann's face was open, fragile—

parts were chipped as on a recovered fresco.

Above her gray head,

a garish postcard of the Emmaus scene,

the colors off, as if painted by numbers, with no concern for
    shading—

its style had a Catholic institutional look.

There it hung, askew in its golden drugstore frame.

It was the scene from the end of Luke, the two disciples,

one named Cleopas, the other anonymous,

forever mumbling Christ's name, and with them,

the resurrected Christ masquerading as a stranger.

They were on their way to that town, Emmaus,

seven miles out from Jerusalem,

gossiping about the impress of Christ's vanishing—

they argued about whether to believe what they had seen;

they were restless, back and forth the debate went—

where there is estrangement there is little peace.

II

Every time we met, Sister Ann prayed first.
At times, my recollections blurred
or a presumption would reverse.
Sister Ann told me Durell was with me *still*,
in a more intimate way than when he lived.
She frequently lost her equilibrium,
as older people sometimes do,
before settling into her worn-out chair
where she listened to me, week after week.

The day I met Durell, I said, the morning light was clear,
startling the town with ornament.
The steeple of Christ Church held the horizon in place,
or so I imagined, as if it had been painted first
with confident amounts of titanium white
before the rest was added. Trees clattered.
The reiterating brick puzzle of Cambridge brightened—
Mass Ave, Mount Auburn, Dunster, Holyoke—
proclaimed a new September,
and new students trudged the streets.
Every blood-warm structure was defined with relief.

Hours before, while the moon's neck wobbled on the Charles
like a giraffe's, or the ghost of a giraffe's neck,
I imagined Durell labored, having slept only a few hours,
caged in his worries of doctor bills, no money,
and running out of people to ask for it:
mulling over mistakes, broken love affairs—
a hospital orderly, a man upstairs,
he probably mumbled unkind epithets about blacks and Jews,
even though the men he loved were blacks and Jews.
Some of his blasphemies, if you want to call them that,
embarrassed me in front of Sister Ann,
but she seemed unflappably tolerant.

At sixty, he was unemployable.
He had taught school and guarded buildings,
each job ending worse than the last.
His refrain was always: "It is not easy being an impoverished
    aristocrat."
He spoke with the old Harvard accent,
I can *still* hear it, I will probably *always* hear it,
with New York City, the North Shore, and the army mixed in,
the *a*s broadened, the *r*s flattened, the *t*s snapped—
so a sentence would calibrate to a confident close,
like "My dee-ah boy, *that* is *that*."
He lived at 19 Garden Street in a rent-controlled studio

on the second floor, number 25;

he said the 25 reminded him of Christmas.

At eleven o'clock,

he probably pulled on his support hose,

increasing the circulation in his legs, blotched green and black.

Next, he would have locked the door with his gold key

and moved deliberately, his smile beleaguered.

Bowing to Miss Littlefield in the landlord's office

at the building's dark cubbyhole of an entrance:

they probably spoke of Queen Elizabeth II,

her disappointments, for Miss Littlefield and he were Royalists
     both.

Then Durell began moving towards me, entering the Square.

Breathing heavily, he might have passed the Brattle

advertising *Judgment at Nuremberg*—

inside the shut black theatrical box the world repeated the past:

Maximillian Schell interrogated Judy Garland and Montgomery
     Clift,

and Marlene Dietrich let the phone ring and ring.

Maybe he passed the Store 24 sign, bright orange,

passed Nini's Corner, where sex magazines were stacked like a
     cliff.

Maybe, maybe. But, maybe not.

Maybe he went another way.

Then I recalled how the T shook that place,

the subway grates pushing up the scent of rat-life and all

   things fallen,

mixing with Leavitt & Peirce exuding its masculine snuff.

Down Plimpton Street he might have gone, past the Grolier,

which I always remembered, for some reason, as closed,

gilded with spines of poetry books for its reredos.

Yes, he probably, most likely, certainly, did that.

Sister Ann wondered if I thought he paused.

I thought not—

poetry offered him no solutions.

At twelve o'clock,

the chairperson called our AA meeting to order.

We called ourselves "The Loony Nooners,"

and met in a Lutheran church basement.

We ate salads out of Tupperware,

shaking the contents like dice to mix the dressing.

Some knitted. Schizophrenics lit multiple cigarettes.

Did they allow us to smoke in the meeting then?

I could not remember.

Either the room was laden with a fog of incense

from all those cigarettes that made our eyes smart

or the church had begun to ask us to go outside.

If that was the case,

we would have seen one another clearly
as if for the first time.
I could not remember now,
I said to Sister Ann, for this was almost thirty years ago.

Didn't acne-pocked Kate want to be a model?
Didn't Electroshock Mike read paperbacks,
and didn't an Irish professor named Tom
welcome Tellus, who could not get over Nam?
I think so. That all sounded right.
Darkened figures in the poor light,
we looked like the Burghers of Calais,
and smelled of brewed coffee, smoke, perfume, urine, human
    brine.
We were aristocrats of time:
"I have twenty-one years," "I have one week," "I have one day."
I have often thought we were like first-century Christians—
a strident, hidden throng, electrified by a message.
Or, another way of thinking of us
is that we were inconvenient obstacles
monetarily removed, much to the city's relief.
From each window well, high heels and business shoes hurried
    past.
Durell H., as he was known to us, took his place,
his thick hair fixed as the waves of an 1800s nautical painting

(perhaps he kept it set with hair spray?),
his Tiffany ring polished to a brilliance,
he set himself apart in his metal folding chair.
He had the clotted girth of Hermann Göring.
What was he thinking about?
Was he thinking about blood clots and possible aneurysms?
Imperious, behind prism-like trifocals,
he quietly said to me, "I've grown as fat as Elizabeth Taylor."

III

The meeting ended and Durell folded his metal chair.
He hated his Christian name—
"Durell," he said. "Who names their child Durell?"
Moving among the crowd, listening to success and failure,
he passed out meeting lists, literature, leaflets.
Durell sponsored men he referred to as "pigeons."
I met him that day. I was his last.

After that, every day we spoke on rotary phones.
I was young and spoke as if my story was the only one.
I told him I had underlined key passages in Plato's *Symposium*,
told him I had been graded unfairly on Dante's *Inferno* and
    Purgatorio,
told him my schedule might not allow for the *Paradiso*.
He matched my telling with listening, advising,
and more listening, mostly over the phone,
and the more he listened the more he was alone.
"Why was that?" Sister Ann asked.
It was some sort of offering, perhaps.
At times, it seemed he needed to guarantee a pardon,

that old Catholic idea of indulgences

lurked somewhere there unspoken,

as if he believed a larger offering might guarantee a larger

pardon.

Such a task demanded his increased singleness.

Yes, that was true. Or was it?

I had trouble settling on the right words with Sister Ann.

Many of my words were not exactly right, the syntax awkward.

I kept having trouble translating Durell, so much I guessed.

How to know?

(Why hadn't I asked him more questions?

He wasn't the sort that invited questions, I *do* remember that.)

Another way of saying it was that when he was with me,

on the phone, then and only then did he seem to move in truth,

and in his truths, reprimanding and hard,

he was made more singular. Maybe that was it.

Whatever the case, he listened, he listened to me.

I missed his listening.

Listening, Sister Ann said, is a memorable form of love.

After the meeting, he gave me his calling card.

The cards were placed inside his compulsively polished silver

card case,

the black capitals raised on their ecru background,

containing his name, bracketed by a "Mr." and a "Jr."—

the "Mr." denoting lost civility,
the "Jr." tallying a lineage that did not bridge.
As we walked down Church Street, the bells of St. John the
    Evangelist rang.
The road was bright, the road full.
Behind the brown gate with the thick black rusted latch,
the monks sang, "It is well, it is well, with my soul, with my
    soul."
We peered in at bookshop clerks locating titles,
watch repairmen bent over lit ocular devices, fixing movements,
florists, hands wet, arranging stems and broken branches.
We saw ourselves reflected.
I laughed with deference, the way a student laughs before a
    teacher.
His skin was flecked with milk blues, lead whites, earthen reds.
In dress and demeanor, he was as rigid as a toy soldier,
for he was part of the republic,
atrophied, with standards, devoted to order.

Everyone found him impossible,
including, at times, me.
Of queers, his word for what he was, but could not admit to,
he said, "You know in the army they could never be trusted."
I mentioned romantic love.
In profile, a silhouette, he paused.

He said, "It has been very vexing, indeed."
By his tone, I knew never to ask again.
A decorum of opprobrium kept him whole,
and so he guarded himself with intensity.
Maybe, Sister Ann suggested, he was guarding me.

Durell said: "I've whittled my world down to no one,
Spencer, with the possible exception of you."

"What happened then?" Sister Ann asked.

He excused himself with a handshake,

his palms soft as bread dough

from all the Jergens he had slathered on,

and then he probably returned to his ambry of a studio,

a place where I would be one of his only visitors.

Although he handed out his number, he did not always answer.

I remember . . . (What do I remember?)

I was free to turn away, but the moment I looked back,

Durell would come back to me,

waiting for me. It seems to me now, after all this time,

few things have as much fidelity as the past.

I remember he had nailed memorabilia above his head

as one would place stones to fortify a castle:

a photograph of him in the army, liberating people, undoing

   Russian codes;

a framed marriage license from England

(although the marriage failed, he often mumbled her name);

his framed diploma, Harvard, and over the corner hung

his graduation cap's faded black tassel.

Next to his pill bottles, an Edward VIII coronation mug he
    doted on,

commemorating an event that never took place.

Maybe he made a bread and bologna sandwich.

Maybe he stepped over the rolled-up tag-sale carpet and drew
    the shades.

By late evening, he might have jotted down notes about God,

obedient as he was to the twelve steps of AA.

He might have written in his tightly looped feminine
    penmanship,

informed by the Palmer Method,

and later repeated a phrase or two to me over the phone.

Or maybe he read from his *Twenty-Four Hours a Day* book

to find a rule maybe, or to search for a sanctuary.

Or maybe he listened to the Reverend Peter Gomes on the
    radio,

the Plummer Professor of Christian Morals at Harvard,

for he often mentioned how he loved the preacher's parallel
    constructions,

yes, maybe he did that, maybe, possibly he did that.

And then, perhaps, he slept,

before the whole routine began once more

with support hose, hair spray, Miss Littlefield, sex magazines,

the Grolier, the folding chair, the meeting, the calling card.
How crazy America was, he said, how he wanted to leave,
but he never left town, except jolting trips to the hospital
in an ambulance down all those brick roads.

V

I lived in Cambridge two years.

After that, wherever I moved, we spoke,

daily, over the phone, on landlines—

talking and listening, listening and talking, for *fifteen* years:

"You all right?" "Yes. You?"

In all that time, I saw him only once more,

and by then he was nearly blind.

In all that time, we barely touched one another.

Why our relationship required its rood screen,

I could not fully explain to Sister Ann,

indeed, I can never seem to properly explain it to anyone.

But I have tried, and I will probably always keep trying.

But if I get nothing right,

I must try to get this nuance of our friendship

and his sponsorship right—

we were bound, bound by a vow, a vow of attention

(there are many causes for attention, among them redemption).

Our attention concerned the spirit,

although that sounds pious and we were not so pious,

we were more selfish, more human than pious.

What else can I say?
I needed a liberator
and liberators can come in some unexpected guises.
I may never wholly explain the two of us.
Perhaps the spirit defies the human mind,
even after all my time with Sister Ann.

Finally, from a hospital, came the report of Durell's last day.
A charge nurse said: "I touched the gangrene leg,
pink flesh was coming back."
His compliments had increased the more his life failed.
In the final week, he quoted Cole Porter songs to me—
*You're a Bendel bonnet, a Shakespeare sonnet, you're Mickey
     Mouse . . .*
I did not repeat the rhymes to Sister Ann.
Who Durell was and why he did what he did and why he hid
what he hid I kept asking her.
Sister Ann quoted from Deuteronomy:
"I set before you life and death . . . choose life."

Old pigeon flying back,
when I arrived at the hospital his body was gone.
The formalities were few,
for he had become a ward of the state.
The staff gave me a brown grocery bag of his things:
a roll of dimes, a pair of shoes, a belt buckle,

an Einstein quote (something about mediocre minds).
Afterwards, I went through Cambridge and found the meeting
    gone.
Night was coming,
Blindness worked on the people, shops, churches, streets.
No one knew me.
People said: "Where will we go?" and "What will we eat?"
I thought I recognized this or that face, but, no, no, too much
    time had passed.
On Church Street, restaurants had replaced bookstores.
Windows on Mass Ave shone with chandeliers.
Someone backed up photographing with a flash.
"Hold still," someone said. "Hold still."
A new set of homeless people pleaded,
coins rattled inside the used coffee cups they shook.
Everyone moved with packages, briefcases, textbooks, flash
    cards, cell phones, flowers.
The Charles advanced, determined as a hearse,
its dark waters gathering up every unattached thing.
An umber, granular dusk-light fell on the elms over Harvard
    Yard
as they swayed dark and slow
like the chords in the waltz from Copland's *Rodeo*.
There I stood, unsure of which way to go.
The light had more ghosts in it
as it must have had that day in Emmaus.

VI

Suddenly, Sister Ann announced our last meeting.

Down the linoleum hallway,

Sister Katherine and Sister Ruth moved and prayed.

Their numbers had dropped from seven to six,

and the nuns decided the Retreat House would close.

Soon the chapel and offices would be leveled

and replaced with condominiums.

In the halls, the swoosh-snap of duct tape yanked, pulled, and
   cut,

straps tightened, vans bleating, and backing up into the back,

weather reports exchanged with the movers.

Sister Ann told me about herself that final time:

parents dead, alcoholic brother dead,

the brother embarrassed she had been a nun.

She opened her Bible on the shipping box between us,

leaned in, her hearing aids on, her silver crucifix knocking on
   her chest.

Above her head, a nail where the Emmaus scene had hung.

I asked: "What caused him to remain?"

Why did he want freedom for me?

Sister Ann spoke then of the Gospel of John
and the Samaritan woman at the well,
the one married nearly as many times as Elizabeth Taylor
and how when Christ listened to her she became the first
    evangelist.
It was Christ's longest conversation with anyone, Sister Ann
    said.
The Samaritan woman's life changed because Christ listened.

John K., from the meetings, dead now too, once said:
"Oh, I knew Durell. He was odd. But we're all odd, you know."
All I know now
is the more he loved me, the more I loved the world.

VII

I lost track of Sister Ann.
I have often thought about her and all the time she spent
   with me.
I have wanted to tell her now for some time
that not long after the cloister closed, Durell's sister located me,
leaving a message on my answering machine
(it was still the time of answering machines),
inviting me to her winter house in Boynton Beach.

Durell's sister gave me directions.
She was quite near to me, as it turned out.
She had some of Durell's belongings that she wanted me to have.
"There isn't much," she said.
"But still, I think you should have what's here."
Durell spoke of his sister often,
but I did not know his family.
However, when we met, we recognized each other
as one sometimes recognizes what one has never seen before.

I said to her: "He knew me better than anyone."
The sentence surprised us.

We sat by the pool in her gated country club.
The Florida evening was a watercolor in the making,
colors bleeding into striking mistakes.
After all the members withdrew,
she said: "There are many things you do not know about my
    brother."
A worker folded terry-cloth towels under a bamboo hut.
Her voice halted as voices halt
when words have been withheld.
"They called him names," she said. "A nancy boy, a priss,
    a sissy, a fairy . . ."
The pool's pulses ceased
until the silence about us was the silence of a palace.

Light disappeared everywhere.
The sun fell. She looked away,
said that he'd been to the army language school,
learned German and Russian, played the organ in his spare
    time,
mentioned he'd taken music with Copland at Harvard
(he had received a "gentleman's *C*"—
the *C* stood for Copland, she said he always said—
which made us laugh and seemed to beckon him to us).
He had hoped for an army career, she went on,
and then she mumbled something about one night,
something happening in a little German town,

I think she said it was in Schleswig-Holstein, near Lübeck,
where he was stationed while borders were being redrawn
(I can't remember the name of the town now),
the army, the men doing something to him, the letters stopping,
   the drink . . .
and then her words fell and sank
into subtle variations of all that goes unsaid.

We heard the distant sound of a train on its track,
crossing the Florida map going brown then black.
He became difficult, isolated—
she spoke softly then like the penitent.
He was always asking for money.
As his requests persisted she began to screen her calls.
"It became easier to tell him I had not been home," she said.
His behavior was affecting her marriage.
She chose never to introduce her children to Durell.
Perhaps he had a mental illness, perhaps he invented—
perhaps, perhaps, perhaps—
but no, she pressed on, perhaps it *was* his sexuality, he was
   too sensitive . . .
"People can be cruel," she said.
She felt he had never adjusted to cruelty
as if cruelty was something that one needed to adjust to.
Later, he was picked up for charges of soliciting sex.
And the more she told me, the less I knew.

All about us, a stillness began to displace the light
and Durell was there, and no longer there, staining the stillness.
After an estrangement ends there comes a great stillness,
the greater the estrangement the greater the stillness.
Across the parking lot, a gate rattled.

I told her he often said his life had been a failure,
I tried to convince him otherwise, but he never believed me.
Half a century ago, she broke off contact.
Her protracted estrangement made her look ill.
"Please, please," she said.
Her voice trailed off,
although what she was pleading for was not clear.
No, no, she did not want her grandchildren to know.
Subtle variations of Florida evening light withdrew with finality.
The pool brightened with moonlight, the color of snow.
The pool was still.
Darkness spilled everywhere.

There we were,
a man and a woman sitting in cushioned lounge chairs—
as if the world would always be
an endless pair of separated things.
We did not touch each other.
We were still a long time.

THE PRODIGAL SON

"Fly at once!" he said. "All is discovered." —Edward Gorey

For A. J. Verdelle

In Miami, this May afternoon, I look up,
the sky hot, so hot, always, and heating up hotter—
how long I have loved this scene.
The clouds are white optimistic churches;
I cannot number them.
Herons, pelicans, and gulls glide like dreams
through cloud portals, cloud porticos, and cloud porte cocheres
Giotto could have done
with his passion for blues and dimensions.
Hard not to love a place always called by possibility.
Nearby, Cuba is singing and somewhere here
Richard Blanco is writing his poems.
As I enter the city,
my bishop walks with a cane towards our cathedral.

The sun shines on the people
and unites us in a delirium of light.
High above this bleached, scorched, fragile, groin-scented
    peninsula,

birds track their insects and remain loyal to their nests.
I look up and I feel bliss building
as I did when my father read another book to me,
and another, the pages like wings.
There are moments of memorable patience in this world.
Airplanes advance towards Miami International,
carrying Jewish retirees and Cuban émigrés—
their descending engines disrupt the white-gloved illegal waiters
at the country clubs in Coral Gables, who deliver flan
to ladies who have pulled skin behind their ears like gum.

This is a place where few decisions are doubted.
On South Beach,
where everyone rearranges or expands their sexual parts,
there seems to be no life outside the physical and time
becomes a tricky thing here, spring looks like winter,
winter like spring, the scenes dense, shifting, shut—
and before you know it the rats have preached from the
     mangoes
and then chewed them into corpses.
And look how the interior decorators
unroll their fresh bolts and wink-wink to new clients—
what would be considered frivolous anywhere else
is here pondered and coerced at great length.
The feminine gains strength.

Moving closer to the cathedral,

the sea presses the harbor, wanting to be loved,

pushing up the cruise ships with its muscles.

The sea says: "I am the sea."

We have seen Cubans arrive atop dolphins' backs here.

Mothers have drowned for their sons,

but the cool gray backs of the dolphins have buoyed their

    children to us,

numbed by the lullaby of sonar clicks.

The sea blesses the city the way mothers do—

forceful, pushy, ungraspable, persistent.

Black mangrove shoots take root on the porous chalky rock,

building themselves up like steeples. Listen.

How the waves love what does not love them back.

Pedicurists buff the toenails of the sugar daddies in the Delano.

Lincoln Road refines its scarlet seductions.

Bees are sticky with tourism inside the motel rooms of the rose.

Red-orange petals from the Royal Poincianas tint the minutes

with flamboyance. Fuchsia bottlebrush blossoms

explode with seeds. I will always love my time in this city,

you might say craziest of cities,

delivering its youth in short shorts

and Rollerblades with rainbow sweatbands.

City smelling of unzipped things.
I do not think the city will ever be mine.
Beautiful Spanish and broken English spoken everywhere.
How I love that sound,
for it is the sound of people making their way
where they were not born.
Maids from Honduras push their carts,
stacking their wrapped soaps,
their cuticles sting with disinfectant,
perspiration staining their uniforms.

O Miami!
For a decade I did not speak to my parents.
Are you listening to me?
I will not bore you with details.
Instead, I will tell you something new.
Listen to me. I was angry.
But the reasons no longer interest me.
I take the liberty of assuming you approve of forgiveness,
stressing hardening gentleness as you do.
I speak to my bishop about my call and the sacraments,
we discuss absolutions, blessings, consecrations—
our work of the soul. The soul has no sex and I am relieved
to speak of a thing alive in the world that has no sex.

The bishop places a paperweight atop my reports on his desk,
our professional talk is measured by the silence of the dead
who are always flinging open their shutters,
religion being the work of the living and the dead,
the hope and release of children turning to their parents—
all that business in life that remains unrehearsed.
Superior to obedient, we pray.
The laughter of the bathers
through the grillwork of the office window pleases me,
their movements rinsed in the baptism of the sea, the
    languorous sea.

The sky at the end of the city trembles.
Light and dust warm to cream to pink to lavender.
Miami, it has been a gorgeous day, indeed. Thank you.
How I love your decks, bridges, promenades, and balconies—
the paraphernalia of connection.
How fast the pastels encroach upon the edges.
I have a dinner engagement in Coral Gables at Books & Books
where I will see the poet Richard Blanco.
I hope he will tell me stories of his beloved, broken Cuba.
Nearly five o'clock now, and I am late.
When I arrive, Richard Blanco speaks of Cuba
as I had wished, and the city quiets all around him.
I think, If our bodies house our souls, Richard,

then poets are the interior decorators of the mind.
Richard Blanco is saying something about going back,
his relatives *singing* poems in the fields. I listen.
Nearby, in the palmatum,
at the Fairchild Tropical Botanic Garden,
the Elephant, Date, Malaysian, Kiwi, Coconut, and Royal
    palms
ask the city to remember their names with the insistence of
    priests.

Goodbye, Miami, goodbye.
Goodbye to the workers laying down the grids of the concrete
    embeds
on the high-rises, reinforcing their masculine nests,
gluing glass with their spermy compounds to stone and steel.
Goodbye to you, South Beach.
Let your rapturous sands darken to a deep grape color.
Let the polished feet of youth launch into their surprises and
    swaps.
Let the elements cool.
Goodbye, Richard Blanco, goodbye.
Today my candidacy for Holy Orders was affirmed.
I listen to the sea flatten.
Cuba pleads in the distance one more night.
Honduras waits on too many things to count.

I can stand still no longer.

Stars smooth the sea with their immaculate highways of long
   lights.

Mother and father,

forgive me my absence.

I will always be moving quietly towards you.

HARTFORD

Visions

For Louise Glück

Hartford, the city that never succeeded like Boston.

✦

City of gunshots, where Hartford Hospital on Jefferson Street employed my mother, a nurse, dressed in her white uniform with pearl buttons, and now employs me, forty-five years later, a chaplain with a black shirt and a white clerical collar. Some nights when I sleep in the on-call room, I think I hear them page my mother's elegant name, Loretta. "Trouble," a nurse says. "Why is the city so troubled?" The nurse checks her patients, each in his or her starched crèche. Observing how the nurses run this place, how they hold much of it together, I have come to criticize my mother less.

✦

The mother walks unsteadily, holds on to her son's arm, afraid of the ice. "I can't wear heels anymore," she says as their liturgy begins. Wallace Stevens is the verger, disappearing behind his poems—silent parents not spoken to and a wife in misery. For a thurifer, a chain-smoking grandmother. Towards the end of our procession of ghosts, the apostle Paul— a Jew, a Benjamite, a maker of tents, who sent his letter, eager to convert, angry when people were not listening to him. "You are not listening to me," my mother says. I spoke to my mother with love, then with anger when she was not listening. "Spencer, is there anything you regret?" "Now that I am older, I would have been kinder to my mother."

✦

Hartford, city of my birth, to you I return and turn to with love. The mother and her son drive by houses they know but do not touch. When they arrive at the cemetery, they move among the graves to show love; they look as if they've come to solve something. But love, love, can it ever be solved? What happens when I say our love may require ignorance? What happens then?

✦

On the day I was born, Martin Luther King, Jr., proclaimed his dream—103-year-old Ada Copeland, the last slave surviving, listened. Nine o'clock on Sunday for the Lithuanian Mass at Holy Trinity at 53 Capitol Avenue. *O Mary, mother of Christ, guard me with maternal care.* My grandmother listened to the black man's dream beside my bassinet, painting her nails fire-engine red on Seymour Street. I weighed ten pounds, the largest baby in the nursery, so large that after I was born, my grandmother came to the hospital and said to my mother: "Loretta, did you have the baby yet?" Years pass. My grandmother settles into her dementia, one last white woman in a black neighborhood, retrieving her past; she grew so familiar with her past that it replaced everything else. Jamaicans moved in, playing Bob Marley. My grandmother chain-smoked, a factory of herself, until the smoke obscured her. When I could see her, her cloud of white hair receding, my grandmother resembled George Washington with lipstick.

✦

Keep awake! Out of Egypt and on into Canaan the Jews went. So, too, with us, this long nervous dislocation. Mary, Mary, my grandmother, where have you gone? We ask your prayers for the following persons who have died: *Mary, James, Richard, John. Pray for those who have died.* Paul, a Jew, who did not like Jews, came to a people divided: those who were with Christ were with him; those who were not were not. But who can be so certain in this world? Edith Stein's becoming a Carmelite nun angered her Jewish family. After she converted, her family stopped speaking to her. During the war, the family was separated and Stein became the guardian of her sister, Rosa, who had the mind of a small child. In August of 1942, a deportation to Auschwitz took place from Westerbork. The two sisters were selected for deportation. They passed through landscapes they had known as children. The train stopped in their hometown of Breslau. Stein stood there as the door slid open, wishing to see the view one last time. She pointed out familiar details to Rosa. The Red Cross reported that the transport had no survivors. Among the names on the transport list was Edith Stein.

✦

In the graveyard we cannot find our dead. Snow erases the names. How ridiculous do we look, not knowing where our dead are? Maybe some of the black families are here? They, who moved up from the South, where four thousand were lynched, who put their coins in the hands of the bus drivers. Mary McLeod Bethune walks here with us, for the longer we walk the more ghosts we collect, she who walked into the White House for tea, invited by Mrs. Roosevelt, and did not see one black face: a call can be a lonely thing.

✦

Round and round Pulaski Circle we went. Can you hear the displaced sing? Under their satin ceilings, the dead repeat their endings in their plush basements, their tongues flat as old wallets. The Puritans said there was no fire to be found under the ice, but I find that to be wrong: where I have found ice I have found fire. In her diary Bethune wrote: "My life has been a spiritual thing." In Mount Olive Church on 20 Battles Street, the dark women are singing: *Glory, glory, hallelujah! Since I laid my burden down. Glory, glory, hallelujah! Since I laid my burden down.* The gold-leaf Roman dome of the Gothic capitol, confused by styles, asks: "Why were my former days better than these?" Quietly, a certain people scatter and disperse with secrets.

✦

Do you believe, you and I, in the death of our Egyptians? Stevens, you do not talk about yourself in your poems, and yet you tell us everything. You slept in Hartford while my grandmother wept on the other side of town, her husband and son dead within months of each other. As you wrote your poem about the jar, my mother went to work as a mail girl at the Fuller Brush Company. As you opened your mind for us, my mother went to visit her father on Mulberry Street. She says: "If you write of my father, do it with respect."

✦

The Connecticut River bounds, gushes, sears the freshets, grays the banks of a garbage-filled birch thicket. The sun is a coin rolling across the ice floes. We drive past Wilson, Windsor, Poquonok Avenue. Long ago, missionaries tore down the sacred lodges of the Mohegans; now their casinos brighten the land like comic strips. *They have healed the wounds of my people lightly, saying: "Peace, peace," when there is no peace.* Birds' claws clamp onto the wires. Together we watch blue jays erupt in a dash of blue wings, blurring my grandmother's backyard to blue. My mother says: "When I was young we would say, 'That's my wedding.'"

✦

Passing beneath the sign "The Dead Shall Be Raised," erected upon faux-Egyptian granite columns, here is my mother, visiting the graves in their snowy ruins. Regard her, for she, like the city, was young once. "Do not say that I was beautiful once and now am old," the mother says to the poet, "Do not say that." And so the poem changes like the snow: the snow is white and black like the universe it came from. Hartford listens down the cemetery's long corridors. *How lonely sits the city that once was full of people.* Below the coffins are thick with facts like filing cabinets; some of the facts are correct, some misplaced, as the dead settle into their final category of aging, becoming a repository of mystery.

✦

Perhaps the city waits for a missionary of some sort? The city has been waiting so long for a voice, it is no longer certain whose voice it is waiting for.

✦

Why do you make me see wrongdoing and look at trouble? A Puerto Rican mother weeps, her stabbed son intubated before us. Fluorescence illuminates their pietà of pumps and wires. "Help us, Father," someone says to me in the confusion of EMTs and doctors administering CPR. How brave my mother must have been attending to those about to die. The pink dawn sky bruises the dilapidated Federalist steeples. They work on the boy all night long. My mother said: "Do you believe Christ really rose from the dead? Church every Sunday, don't you think that's a bit excessive?" When I travel to Jerusalem, I send a postcard from Yad Vashem. "Dear Mom," it begins, "I am here." A forgiving snow falls on the mother and the son. By the end of my shift, I write in the chart: "The boy died this morning at 6 AM."

✦

In the cemetery, my mother asks: "And what will you put in your book?"

✦

Smoke-colored, my grandmother's house has stucco embedded with ground glass like in a kaleidoscope. Inside there was a crucifix above each door, each Christ jaundiced from my grandmother's Viceroys. My mother says: "Do not rush your mother, these are my memories, one day you will be old too." The mother and son understand each other well and not so well.

✦

Maybe here? No. Over here. Where? Bless James Witkins, the father, who parked his car on Pearl Street with his crutch, not yet adjusted to his stump, dying before they cut the second leg off. Bless Richard Witkins, the twenty-four-year-old son, who died in a car accident weeks later, identified through dental records. Bless Richard's baby, Laura-Lynn, left behind, screaming and teething in my mother's arms. Mourners delivered gladioli. My mother says: "I hate that flower." Bless my grandmother who would not get out of bed. *Do you work wonders for the dead? Will those who have died stand up and give you thanks?* "I cannot remember that year," says my mother. But who forgets a year?

✦

"You do not understand your mother," my mother says. Wasn't there an argument under the pull chain in the kitchen?

Isn't that what my mother has said for years? Didn't Mr. and Mrs. Witkins emphatically shut the venetian blinds? Isn't that how my mother described it? Their children were in the field, *yes*, there were fields. They were immigrants who came over on boats counting coins and speaking in their dying language. I have heard the story a hundred times. Didn't my grandmother turn to her husband and say: "Are you a Jew?" *They said nothing to anyone, for they were afraid.*

✦

We move towards the thrift of the dead. Hours accrue in their closed teeth. We walk towards an economy of subtraction. Carbon, hydrogen, oxygen, and nitrogen leave one body for another. In Sage-Allen's collections department, my grandmother worked with a bank of ladies tallying the sum of things and on their hands were wedding rings. The house where my mother was born is a hair salon. Above the door, the sign reads: "African Braiding & African Movies." Around the windows, Christmas lights blink. I was not here to bury my grandmother. Anger divided my mother and me and we were not speaking. It seems foolish now. Still, the city welcomes me even though I have been a fool. Once again the mother says something about the Jews, unkind it seems to the son, given her father's mysterious history, but as the son knows, it is not easy to love what you might be. My mother's father died when she was twenty. "Too young," she says. "Too young." All her life she has searched for her father. How to find a man when all the records have been misplaced?

✦

"Cold, cold. It's cold," says the son. Where is the Royal Typewriter, the American Rifle, the bicycle and piano factories? Tobacco sheds lean, abandoned. Egyptians will lie dead upon the shore. Beyond the plot, in the city, the priests have no people. What of the last name, Witkins? When I travel to the Hall of Names at Yad Vashem, the records show every Vitkin and Witkin shot in a ditch outside Vilnius. When I call my mother from Jerusalem, to speak of what I have found, she says: "I have often thought . . . I have often thought . . ."

✦

"Fire! Fire!" the citizens screamed under the big top. It was 1944, the war was not over, and my mother was a young girl. A cool breeze blew across her face as it does in summer evenings in Jerusalem. She said: "You could smell the burning flesh all over the city." The tent, dipped in paraffin, went up in seconds from a cigarette tossed. Adults passed children over their heads until they were overcome. People were trampled to death at the exits. The camels were silent as they burned. Some graves belong to the fire: Baby Thelma, The Fat

Girl. Stevens never mentioned the fire; instead he wrote: "This has always been the toughest time of year for me. I want to give the office a kick." Our presence is no nuisance to the dead. The dead know disappointment beyond remedy. My grandmother listened to King as she rocked me: "I may not get there with you. But I want you to know tonight, that we, as a people, will get to the promised land."

✤

Mrs. Stevens stood behind the soup tureen, lonely, waiting to take a second nap. Although her newly baptized husband lay dying at Hartford Hospital, Mrs. Stevens refused to visit him in his last days. Maybe Mrs. Stevens is here in the graveyard? She who posed for the dime? Although it is a large cemetery, it is hard to tell who is important.

✤

Hartford, come and see the graves overrun as doormats. Hartford, follow them like a Shakespearean fool. Often now, my mother speaks to the dead, the parade that has marched since heaven and hell began. Snow flocks the windshield of our car, the wipers scrape like a finger searching a text or a hand pulling the morgue sheet back.

✤

"What will your mother think now that the poem is done?" The light makes a daguerreotype of Hartford Hospital. Snow falls over the mother and her son, cloaking them in dark whites. The moon rises, sheets Bushnell Park. Stevens wrote that the poet does not yield to the priest. But religion and poetry, can they ever be divided? Then he ignored his daughter once more, preferring thought to people. Hartford, where have you gone? Have you disappeared like Palestine? "Hartford," someone says on the train. "Who lives there now?" In its history, no one has ever taken a vacation to Hartford. I work the Christmas shift. A black grandfather, Moses, dies in the Red Pod. The family is large, twenty or thirty strong. "Pray for us, Father," someone says. What ignites the passion for worship like disappearance?

✦

"Tell me the story about your father," says the son. The mother tells the story the son has heard many times: "Once, in Lithuania, I traveled to the square in Vilnius. I was looking for a sign of my father. The Russians had changed all the names of the streets so it was hard to find things. For days I saw nothing to remind me of my father. A Russian soldier escorted me around quickly. Then, in the square, above a tailor shop, I saw a flower box, and on the flower box, written in chalk, was my name, 'Loretta.' It was a sign I knew my father was there. I took a picture of it with my camera. My name could not be seen with the naked eye. Only the camera picked it up. See. See. Here is my name."

+

Who can know the story of the one they love most? *I will stand at my watch post, and station myself on the rampart.* Paul wanted to be bound to the good and the pure; where it would lead him he could not be sure. Paul was depending on the story of a Jew he hardly knew. "O, you fools," he said to those not listening. Wallace Stevens, stand here with us, whisper something to us now about angels. Distract us on your flute. Mary McLeod Bethune, record something about hope in your diary. My mother says: "I forgot to tell you something. When you were born, your grandmother came to the hospital and she looked at you and said to me she thought you would be a priest. I forgot to tell you that before. I just remembered it. Your grandmother was Catholic, you know." A poet, like a priest, works with facts and mysteries: the facts mysterious, the mysteries factual. The ER doors fly open with gurneys, X-rays, paperwork, syringes, body maps, intercoms, wallets to find next of kin. In the parking lot, after my shift, a nurse named Janet who likes to joke with me says: "Hey there, sugar, you all right?"

+

For thou art with me; thy rod and thy staff, they comfort me.
Before I finish this poem I travel to Vilnius, the city so many
fled, and when they fled they kept no record, for they were
afraid. In my hand I carry a name for my grandfather. The
Lithuanian State Historical Archives found a name, but it is
not the name I know from the grave, and the dates seem off.
It is a Jewish name. The lady in the records department said:
"Names changed. It was very common. But perhaps he's not
a Jew. Why must he be a Jew? A Jew marrying a Christian
would be very rare." Vilnius flickers before the son with van-
ishing muteness from the church bells to the forest. In 1941,
within six months, they killed two hundred thousand Jews
here; they fell in a ditch in the woods. There were no trans-
ports. I go to the synagogue and the rabbi says: "I, too, was
ashamed to say I was a Jew." The mother says: "He never went
to church, spoke Yiddish, said his records went down in a fire.
He was seventeen, he got on a boat, he never saw his mother
again." She tells the story of the flower box once more. I prom-
ise her to search for more names. Her confusion has defined
me the way confusion defines Jerusalem and my love has re-
quired confusion as religion requires poetry.

+

Mother, love requires that we do not separate. Death has made us earnest. Much of what we love we no longer touch. Yet still we come to love. "Let us go to the cemetery and find our dead," the son had said to his mother. Snow falls over the hospital where the son was born. The snow obscures the city, falls in plumes, like smoke. The son follows his mother into the snow.

12:20 IN NEW YORK

A Sunday, in January,

and I've come to the West Village,

to visit you, my brother, living in this city.

For twenty years you have walked past

the French Roast coffee shop and the Emma Lazarus house,

to different jobs, different bosses.

You never wrote letters or favored the postcard,

even before these faded.

E-mails, cells, landlines,

none of these facilitate our bond.

You prefer the unobstructed moment.

So, here we are.

Recently, you've begun feeding a stray cat on your fire escape—

when you gave the animal a name, the animal became yours.

You called him WAYD, which you told me,

when writing a text, is short for "What are you doing?"

Devotion becomes the most reasonable emotion as we age;

we recognize it in contrast to the losses

and the losses can be defined only with time.

We go uptown, to the Arbus show,

her last photographs, the adults in a state institution

for the mentally handicapped in Vineland, New Jersey—
this was after she divorced, after she stopped believing
in love and started photographing sex clubs.
One of the women in the institution told her:
"I got a boyfriend, he says I'm beautiful.
I told him he hasn't seen the pretty parts."
The subjects wore Halloween masks,
the photographs were untitled.
None of the subjects in the rose garden knew who Arbus was;
this anonymity began to broaden her art.

In a letter to her daughter,
she wrote she had finally captured sunlight.
Her letters were typewritten.
Now typewriters are gone.
Arbus hated making appointments, hated calendars.
She liked the idea of a family album
when thinking of her work,
each member part of a larger group, related, tolerated.
On a postcard, she once wrote: "I think all families are creepy."
Shortly after dinner with her brother,
the poet Howard Nemerov,
she returned to her apartment and slit her wrists.
It was July 1971.
Astronauts floated in the TV.
In Arbus's darkroom at 29 Charles Street,

her contact sheets materialized from their chemicals.
Around that same time, our mother and father
adopted you, my brother, from an unnamed woman
who gave you away. Somewhere a family album holds her.
What is she doing now?
We took you home and we gave you a name.
Although I know the story well, I do not tell it now.
There are stories that separate me from you;
for that reason, I will not tell them.

We go back to the Village,
down Christopher Street,
past sex shops and Chinese massage parlors.
On Hudson, past Saint Luke in the Fields,
we walk past two gay men with a baby in their arms.
My brother, we have fought
and reconciled as brothers do.
If there are things I regret,
the time for regretting is gone.
Handsome man, you speak of your long-term boyfriend
(fifteen years?) and how the two of you have decided to separate.
We talk of museums you frequent:
the Neue Galerie, the Whitney, the Frick, MoMA.

We do not speak of poetry.
Recently, books have begun to disappear.

My brother, if I name the things disappearing from the world,
how long can I keep them from doing so?
At the Caffe Reggio, I study you,
backlit with afternoon sunlight,
the light intersected by taxis, golden retrievers on leashes,
people walking with yellow rain slickers,
messengers on bicycles with orange stripes,
the masses in the city motivated by a hundred forms of touch.

If I once thought love had limits,
I was wrong.
Then, we check the returns on the train schedule.
I enter the subway at Union Square.
Passengers line up like prints hung in a darkroom.
Teenagers send well-thumbed texts on their phones,
as if romance could fit into such a small dungeon.
Air and more air rushes through the tunnels and turnstiles.
Not long after I left,
you texted from your cell—
your cat had run away.
What do we do in this life when what we love
does not come back?
As the train begins its turn towards New Haven,
Harlem goes by in unerring, random snapshots—
negatives, double exposures,
black on white, white on black,

images captured, lost, focused, then lost again.

The sealed train windows fill up with their industry—

life, life, and more life, all kinds.

I never tire of it.

A FEW TENDER MINUTES

10:01 AM

It is a summer of rain and I am a seminarian. I visit the Osborn
State Correctional Facility. The metal gate opens, then closes
behind me, like legs uncrossed and crossed. On the mental
health ward, behind a small meshed window, a naked man,
wrapped in a bedsheet, poses like Constantine crossing the
Milvian Bridge. There is a particular sound in prisons. More
insistent than rain, it is the honeyed sound of the hive, the
sound of men packed in on top of each other, the sound of
regret, anger, and resignation, all beginning and beginning
again. I hear them hum in their cells, sticky, strong from bar-
bells. Then I see them—their skins colored black, brown,
mocha, plum, peach, and white. Intricate tattoos cover the
men like road maps. Semen sweetens the air. A muscular in-
mate's biceps rise from his T-shirt like loaves of bread. His
one-armed boyfriend smokes a cigarette with his hook. We
enter the chapel. My fellow seminarian panics. A nurse rushes
him to her office in a wheelchair.

11:08 AM

We are told the sedated seminarian will not return. Rain messes up Connecticut. Rivers break. Gardens drown. Water collects in the spokes of the spider's web, straightjacketing the flies. In the prison yard, beyond the chain-link fence with razor strips, the landscape runs like a finger painting done by a child. In the thickets, the shadowy traffic of birds in panic. The Carolina wrens have returned to the chokecherry trees— voluble, curious evangelists. The males construct nests with feathers, mud, and twigs. The females inspect and throw out their sticks and sing: "Begin! Begin again!" The male will sing 250 repetitions until a nest can be settled upon. Through the window bars, rain hammers the wrens as they argue over feckless nests.

11:50 AM

The clock is a wheelchair disappearing down the corridor of time. We pray with the inmates in a circle. Allowed a few minutes with each inmate, I have time for two. A sex offender says he has been wrongly accused. How will he return to his mother's house? How to begin again? The guard says, "Next." Before me is a man who does not disclose his crime, a Native American who will be released tomorrow. Something about his expression is reminiscent of Sitting Bull after he won the Battle of Little Bighorn and had entered those rodeo shows with Wild Bill to tour Europe: triumphant resignation begins to describe it, but not completely. For forty years, he tells me, his job has been to greet new inmates, which gave him money for toothpaste and pencils. Behind him, a mural of crude voluptuous angels covers the cinder blocks: their wings and breasts have absorbed the Clorox stink of the place. What prayer is in my book for him? The guard picks at his nail beds with his key. He says: "Two more minutes." My crucifix dangles from my chest like a fledgling.

AMONG SCHOOLCHILDREN

For Father Edmund Harris

The one-story houses were painted aqua, violet, orange,
    pistachio.
I spoke to the taxi driver in broken Spanish.
I was becoming a priest, I told him, God willing—*Soy un*
    sacerdote
(the tense wrong, the article unnecessary, the *r* rolled too
    strong)—
as we drove over ruts, potholes, and alongside hungry dogs.
Much of the taxi's interior had been removed.
Time slowed that summer in San Pedro Sula.
Around the rotary, legless men shook their tambourines,
epileptics convulsed, and the blind tapped their sticks
through donkey excrement. Blue mountains and fields of
    banana trees
shadowed the city's edges. There were the many poor
on the grassless riverbank assembling houses out of rubbish.
I had come to work in the orphanage in Villa Florencia.
Inside the ten-foot wall with barbed wire, behind the metal
    gate,
guards fingered their pistols like Bibles,

and seventy orphaned girls politely greeted strident Christians.

One girl had been found on a coconut truck.

She had lived on coconut juice since birth,

had trouble speaking, preferred not to be held.

Two sisters had been left at a street corner on a sheet of
   cardboard;

their mother told them to wait, then never came back.

It was a landscape both porous and uninviting.

Halfway up one mountain was an enormous white Coca-Cola
   sign.

Rain steadily fell against the tin roofs and colored the chapel
   windows to plum.

Sweat stained my T-shirt the color of a steeped tea bag.

The more I spoke to the girls the more insistent they became,

making fun of my accent, saying in English: "What's my name?
   Say my name."

At night, grease shone on my cheeks, lit by the Coca-Cola sign.

The clock on the nightstand was a face I could not reach.

A world widened in me. But what of my Protestant professors

rearranging furniture in their well-appointed heads,

talking of Hooker and Baxter, hunched in their sepia-colored
   libraries?

In the dark of my room, I pondered them.

Was it true, what they said, that a priest is a house lit up?

THE POOR

By Roberto Sosa, a translation

The poor are many
and so—
impossible to forget.

No doubt,
as day breaks,
they see the buildings
where they wish
they could live with their children.

They
can steady the coffin
of a constellation on their shoulders.
They can wreck
the air like furious birds,
blocking the sun.

But not knowing these gifts,

they enter and exit through mirrors of blood,

walking and dying slowly.

And so,

one cannot forget them.

MY GREAT-GRANDMOTHER'S BIBLE

Faux-leather bound and thick as an onion, it flakes—
an heirloom from Iowa my dead often read.
I open the black flap to speak the *spakes*
and quickly lose track of who wed, who bred.
She taped our family register as it tore,
her hand stuttering like a sewing machine,
darning the blanks with farmers gone before—
Inez, Alvah, Delbert, Ermadean.
Our undistinguished line she pressed in the heft
between the testaments, with spaces to spare,
and one stillborn's name, smudged; her fingers left
a mounting watchfulness, a quiet repair—
when I saw the AIDS quilt, spread out in acres,
it was stitched with similar scripts by similar makers.

THE UPPER ROOM

For Mary Jane Zapp

If you looked up, you might have seen me,
although few saw me in that room:
it required crossing the threshold
from the profane to the sacred,
a paradoxical proposition for most, including myself.
But I went in search of the transcendent in those days,
which required leaving a particular world for another.
It is never easy to abandon a world.
It was my second attempt.
This time I was much older
and the strident faiths of my younger colleagues
often gave me pause.

I lived on the third floor on 363 Saint Ronan Street.
By that time in my life, I recognized the room was temporary—
from the start, I accepted the dwelling's transitory nature.
Each November, between shut gray New England spaces,
I saw nervous birds, those itinerant immigrants,
abandon the trees; addicts of seeing,
they charged the horizon when color was removed.

I pressed against the window
as if it were a museum case,
just as the world pressed against the windows of New Haven,
examining each one of us like a relic with a label,
in the same inquisitive, cursory manner.
The skyline was muted, ill-defined:
New Haven sprawled from Gothic elegance
to poverty without drama.
The landscape was obstructed:
we were deaf to the sea's plainchant, could not smell its stink,
taste its salt, the harbor blocked by a highway and warehouses.
The city favored neither misery nor ecstasy.
Whether our sanctuary could purify the world was debatable.

In my attic room, angled by dormers,
the gloaming laid down golden beams
that lit up the room like a classroom.
At night the room nourished the moon and made it bloom.
I felt tended by the light.
It must have been the maid's room once;
when I heard the floorboards creak
I imagined them accompanied by her singular sighs.
Long ago painters painted over the servant bells and buzzers.
My desk chair, left over from a dining room set,
lurched and had been repeatedly glued, then finally taped—

a promising artifact for a future archeological dig.
The room was like many rooms I had known:
furnished, rented, up flights of stairs,
a chest of drawers with a knob missing, a bed slept in by many—
all indications that things last longer than people.
A lamp, half broken, with an ostrich statue for a stand,
had one red eye, the other eye was missing—
so it had the vantage point of half the world.

On my desk lay *The Book of Common Prayer*,
mine since my confirmation at the age of forty-two,
looking like a grammar book with notes and Post-it stickers,
coffee stains and pencil marks covered the pages
and from the spine,
red, green, and gold streamers like the tails of kites—
that book, structured and defined by time,
from birth to marriage to death—"O God,
whose days are without end, and whose mercies
cannot be numbered: make us, we beseech thee, deeply sensible
of the shortness and uncertainty of life . . ." Sensible?
How to be sensible about uncertainty?

Above my bed, I hung a Byzantine icon of Christ,
a kitschy trinket copied and laminated countless times,
sold in religious gift shops the world over,

originally from Saint Catherine's Monastery at Mount Sinai,

the longest-running monastery

functioning since the sixth century,

the bluish Christ depicted had eyes staring in two directions,

as if Christ had managed his ministry with his eyes crossed.

I had books: C. S. Lewis's *The Great Divorce*,

Gregory of Nazianzus' *Orations*.

After I was ordained a deacon,

my red stole hung over my closet door, signaling an exit.

My life had depended on not being seen.

I needed a hiding place

and that room compensated for such an enterprise.

To the east, two mullioned windows opened on New Haven—

oak, spruce, holly, yew filled in the foreground,

and there, beneath, to the right,

a bed of purpled cornflowers bloomed,

their petals colored like Communion wine,

always ruined before we could cut them for the dinner parties.

Beneath me I could hear a bejeweled hubbub,

the rub and thrum of purple churchy murmurs:

deans, archdeacons, bishops, canons,

postulants, candidates, monks, nuns,

even presiding bishops and past presiding bishops.

A neo-Colonial redbrick house with Italianate flourishes,
on the second floor Palladian windows sparkled like bifocals.
We heard mice and bats in the walls gently tunneling;
they sounded like a hand holding a pen and writing in a diary,
moving forward with blind discovery.

Once grand and private
but now communal, the house passed
from a wealthy family to the Episcopal church,
like the first house church in Dura-Europos,
and we, the seminarians, occupied several rooms,
perpetuating innocence and displaying a command
of the obvious: one repeated,
"We are infiltrating the world we call God's";
another moved with the instinct to help that was misplaced;
another believed the world corrected what was not genuine.

We made meals for one hundred every week,
cleaned toilets, shut doors, did laundry, made beds,
our fingers cut from chopping,
stinging with chemicals, tender from scalding.
Perfunctory, undressing, each of us quiet, cold,
grimly chewing our meals in the twilight,
we did not wish to disturb the dean's family on the second floor.
We were made for any novel by Anita Brookner or Barbara Pym.

At 7:30 AM, in Saint Luke's Chapel,

behind the double doors with frosted glass,

we looked up at the ornate coffered ceiling,

white with delft blues,

its cornices and moldings with curlicues

like the inside of a coffin lid.

Often, we sang the Blake hymn about countenance and
    Jerusalem.

Our fussy rustle of copes, chasubles, surplices, stoles

sounded like birds picking at newspapers.

Inside everyone sat, knelt, stood, and genuflected

with the informed hush of a troupe of mime artists.

The liturgy followed Rite I,

beginning with the Prayer for the Penitent:

Almighty and most merciful Father,

We have erred and strayed from thy ways like lost sheep,

We have followed too much the devices and desires of our own
    hearts,

We have offended against thy holy laws,

We have left undone those things which we ought to have done,

And we have done those things which we ought not to have
    done.

At that moment in time,

much of my family had gone,

rapidly, all at once—
grands, uncles, aunts, even three cousins.
The first spring my father had a heart attack, nearly died.
Another cousin's cancerous esophagus was removed.
The deaths and near-deaths were earthquakes;
even though New England knows few earthquakes,
after each one I was never able to put everything back,
before the next, the next, and the next.
The room's makeshift state reflected my mental disarray:
cast-off shoes, a bureau top covered with misplaced numbers,
and separate currencies—
dollars, euros, pounds, lempiras, sheqalim—
all with portraits of well-fingered human beings.
I had acquired the habits of departure.

The clock's hands scissored the day's indigo shadows.
I practiced homilies.
I strove for brevity.
"Five minutes," the priests instructed me.
Who I belonged to was about to change.

My family had lived and suffered, suffered
in ways not imagined. Of my generation nearly all
had married poorly, and few stayed married long enough
to have children. We were disappearing.

But we who remained kept on, over the phone, mainly:
"John Alexander is marrying at nineteen."
"Aunt Dorothy is ninety-*three*."
When the dead outnumber the living
you remember the living, gently, gently—
using the tone one associates with church pews.
How this one went broke
or that one resented *something*, I stopped recalling.

Three years finished like that.
One last uncle, in a nursing home, in Avon,
senile, in a diaper, a policeman, fed with a spoon by his wife,
a week before he died, held me, would not let go.
At school, we prepared our last meal,
served dishes alert to portions, wiped down the tables.
The way forward was the way out.
The world was adjusting to the quick—
colors, temperatures, people coming, going,
staring at each other, each with a story.
It had been a long winter.
I'd been ordained in a blizzard and now the frost's zodiacs
had all disappeared. This was the world,
and I was still in it. My suitcases packed,
my clerical collars placed in my trunk like bandages.

Downtown, at Yale's British art museum,

visitors observed Whistler's oils,

where British bluish light overtook one wall,

and there the world often lingered,

searching for solace in a scene.

Privately, and secretly,

in the basements of the Beinecke,

librarians in gloves opened the medieval books of hours,

resting them upon foam cradles

for the curious and the concerned.

On vellum pages, unicorns nosed bright blue virgins.

In a classroom, Harold Bloom closed his eyes;

looking like a traveler on board a ship,

he recited D. H. Lawrence and T. S. Eliot.

He was old now, walked with a cane,

had fallen down a flight of stairs.

Should he stop teaching, he wondered aloud, to his students.

But what else would he do?

He preferred Lawrence to Eliot,

could not abide his anti-Semitism.

Undergraduates took notes in their last classes.

All at once, spring stampeded.

Crocuses shot up.

Birds reassumed the air.

Then, graduation.

The rivers of youth reversed.

Maintenance crews lined up the white folding chairs,

and if you squinted, before the ceremony,

the empty chairs looked *exactly* like Arlington National
Cemetery.

As fate would have it,

I was moving far away, to another country.

I awaited what I could not see,

an activity that preoccupies many religious lives.

I crossed the threshold.

The dean's door locked behind me one last time.

Had I chosen it?

Had I chosen it all?

The Benedictine cross around my neck,

given by a friend, was light,

a silver, tarnished, chipped Christ, on shiny onyx,

a man I now relied on—

paradoxically bound and free—

a childless, bachelor Jew, slightly feminine.

HYMN

And after the day was over,
I told my friend Marie this story:

He was a young man and it was finally April.
A piano player played in Washington Square Park.
The young man walked along with the older man.
Daffodil buds unbuckled their gold
in the prosperous dirt-beds wherever the two men looked.
Green applause stirred in the trees.
A woman on the street called out to the older man:
"Beautiful man, you, beautiful man . . ."
The two knew each other
and this coincidence made a bright light.
She spent her days raising doves and squirrels.
How did she support herself?
She observed the two together
and respected the fragility of the moment
as the angel does in Fra Angelico's *Annunciation*.

The young man came to visit the city.
He said he had written in his diary about the older man,
had thought about him since they had lunch the week before,

a lunch the young man suggested.

He gave the older man a CD, all love songs.

The older man had been alone long enough to be reflective.

In the Anglo-Catholic churches that Sunday

deacons would chant the story of Lazarus from the Gospel of
John:

Those who believe in me will live, even though they die.

The young man said to the older man:

"When did you come out?"

They walked through the park. With deliberation,

the older man said: "I could kiss you."

Somewhere, doves settled on the ledges of the woman's
shoulders.

Silence surrounded the men as they went back to a brownstone

and lay on a high four-poster bed.

Before them a painting of a Roman city,

intricate as a symphony, that could have contained them.

Light grew long in the window and across the painting's canvas.

The older man said: "Do you feel like you could kiss me?"

The young man responded,

speaking in a voice that lacked drama,

a voice both kind and bright, and said: "Not now."

The deacons practiced their chanting:

Those who live and believe in me will never die.

Time pressed on the older man.

His passion collapsed.

Things would go unexplored.

The two men felt the folly of the moment.

The young man lingered with nonchalance,

a cruelty that belongs to youth.

Deacons took out their pencils and underlined certain words:

Mary arrived where Jesus was, and as soon as she saw him,
    she fell at his feet.
"Lord," she said, "if you had been here, my brother would
    not have died."

They went to dinner.

A Chinese restaurant on Sixth Avenue.

One they had not planned on.

Another friend of the older man joined them,

a woman who was writing a play with many characters.

She promised to take the young man to Grand Central,

for the young man had never been to the city before.

Suddenly, before they ordered their meal,

through the phosphorescent window

now expanding like a poem,

filling with a throng earnest to go home,

two more men appeared, both middle-aged,

whom the older man knew.

Was it possible he had not seen them in twenty years?

They came to the glass like fish in an aquarium.

What were their names?

Into the restaurant and poem they came.

One had been married to a woman, and had had a child,

and he *did* remember the child's name.

In the sacristies, deacons continued their chanting,

going down a third on the fourth syllable

from the end of every sentence:

He cried with a loud voice, "Lazarus come out!"

The table was full now.

Joy grew in the dark as it had in Jerusalem

two thousand years ago. Silverware glinted.

People opened the caves of their mouths,

laughed so their gold and silver fillings shone,

raised their arms like circuit breakers,

everyone connected by the pleasures of the ordinary life.

(O, the voltage of wants and needs contained in that city!)

Everyone spoke over each other, told jokes.

The waitress recorded everyone's order, distracted.

The two new men announced they were married:
proudly, they showed their rings.
Then it was time for the young man to depart.
The doves must have been sleeping by then.
Everyone stood. The dark street shone with light.
Electricity and stars! Fire, bolts, shards, beams,
shafts, glints, shimmers, matches, cigarettes, sparks!
The deacons were lousy with gospels,
leaving them open all over the city.

"We were free," I said to Marie, "and I was happy.
It didn't matter about the young man."
There was no more time to hate ourselves.
Many had already died and some had been kept from dying.
We spoke of her brother, John,
and we spoke of my cousin John, now both long gone.
It was our time now.
Over the phone, I could hear her daughter, Inan,
asking for dinner in the background,
the daughter that had come to her late in life, a gift.
The Gospel of John was right:
the world holds so much life.
There are not enough books to record it all.
I kissed the young man on his cheek, very lightly.

Jesus said to them: "Unbind him, and let him go."

We each went our separate ways
following where we were being led.
Marie said: "Write it down, just as it happened."

Acknowledgments

Grateful acknowledgment is made to the Florida State Arts Board, the Guggenheim Foundation, the Amy Lowell Traveling Poetry Scholarship, the National Endowment for the Arts, the Two Brothers Fellowship, the Mrs. Giles Whiting Foundation, and the Witter Bynner Fellowship from the Library of Congress, awarded as I wrote this book.

Grateful acknowledgment is made to *The American Scholar*, *Boulevard*, *The New Republic*, *The Massachusetts Review*, *The New Yorker*, *Poetry*, and *Tikkun*, where poems previously appeared.

Grateful acknowledgment to Scribner's for publishing "The Road to Emmaus" in *The Best American Poetry 2012*, edited by Mark Doty.

Gratitude to the Ucross Foundation, The MacDowell Colony, and Richard Blanco for residencies.

Gratitude to Bishop Carlos López-Lozano and his wife, Doña Ana López-Lozano, and the congregation of Catedral del Redentor, who gave me a home in Madrid, Spain.